Playing Orcnestra

by Lauris Shaw
illustrated by Christina Miesen

Harcourt
SCHOOL PUBLISHERS

Cover, 4, 6, 9, 10, 11 ©Photolibrary.com; 13 ©Eitan Simanor /Alamy

Printed in Mexico

ISBN 10: 0-15-350651-2
ISBN 13: 978-0-15-350651-2

Ordering Options
ISBN 10: 0-15-350599-0 (Grade 2 On-Level Collection)
ISBN 13: 978-0-15-350599-7 (Grade 2 On-Level Collection)
ISBN 10: 0-15-357832-7 (package of 5)
ISBN 13: 978-0-15-357832-8 (package of 5)

2 3 4 5 6 7 8 9 10   050   15 14 13 12 11 10 09 08 07

Making Music Together

Do you play an instrument and make music? Do you play alone or do you play with friends?

Making music with other people can be fun. Some people play together in a band. Some people play together in an orchestra. An orchestra is a very large group of musicians. They play music together using different instruments.

Going on a Journey

There is an orchestra in my town.
When I hear the music, I feel like
I am going on a journey. I see
pictures in my head and experience
different feelings.

Instrument Families

Look at all the instruments in the
orchestra. There are four families of
instruments. They are called strings,
woodwinds, brass, and percussion.
Each instrument family has its
own sound.

6

At the front of the orchestra is the string family. The violin is the smallest string instrument. The harp is the biggest. It is bigger than I am!

The woodwind family is behind the string family. The piccolo makes the highest note. It makes me think of a little bird. The contrabassoon makes the lowest note.

The brass family is behind the woodwind family. The brass instruments make the loudest sounds in the orchestra!

The percussion family is right at the back of the orchestra. Listen to the rhythm. Hear the different sounds. The percussion instruments make the music more exciting!

Following the Conductor

Watch the conductor wave his baton up and down, and side to side. He is telling the players how and when to play their instruments.

The players concentrate and watch the conductor. He helps them play with expression. He can make the volume loud or soft. He can make the rhythm fast or slow.

Sometimes the conductor wants just one instrument family to play. Listen to the brass instruments blare!

Sometimes he wants all the instruments to play together. Different sounds blend together into beautiful music.

The Creative Composer

The composer who wrote the music was very creative. Sometimes the music is slow and sad. Sometimes the music is fast and exciting.

After the Performance

I applaud when the music finally ends. The performance was breathtaking. I enjoyed it a lot.

The conductor is relieved that the performance is over. The musicians are pleased they played well. Playing in an orchestra is what they like to do more than anything.

I would like to join an orchestra someday. Making music with a lot of people must be very exciting!